Drugs, Alcohol, and

MEN KILLED ME,

then

GOD HEALED ME

by

Pearl Keith

Fairmont Books is a ministry of The McDougal Foundation, Inc., a Maryland nonprofit corporation dedicated to spreading the Gospel of the Lord Jesus Christ to as many people as possible in the shortest time possible.

Fairmont Books
P.O. Box 3595
Hagerstown, MD   21742-3595

www.mcdougal.org

ISBN 1-58158-007-X

Printed in the United States of America
For Worldwide Distribution

DEDICATION

To my mother, Mrs. Janie Wilson, who has been praying for me for more than twenty years. Oh, how sweet is a mother's love!

Acknowledgments

I am indebted to many people who have helped me over the years. I wish to express a special thanks to a few:

To God, who is the head of my life.

To Rev. Agnes M. Turks, who has helped me through the years.

To Kyle and Donna for being such generous friends.

To the saints at Faith Temple Church in Pittsburgh, Rev. Sharon Leviege, and Minister Patton.

To Bishop Robert Scott Dixon, Elder Renee Dixon, Brian Crumbaker, and Timi Fleming at Salvation Praise Ministries

To Rev. Russell Medley, Sandy McDonald, and Bernice Blue at St. Stephen's.

To Emma Dobbs, Vara Jackson, and Valrie Proctor at Morningstar Church.

To Eunice Johnson, Robbie Riley, and Minister Patricia Thomas at Powerhouse Deliverance.

To Rev. Charles Summer at St. Paul's AME Church and Melonie Spencer at Christian Love Ministry.

To my friends in the Lord: Janice Epps, Thelma Jones, Winsome Meundy, Minister Patricia Neal, and Rev. S.C. Rucker.

To my one and only son, Dwayne K. Ridgeway, and my beloved daughter, Marquetta D. Wilson, with much love, both at Salvation Praise Ministries.

To all my family, especially to my late grandmother, Pearl Bookheart, and last, but not least, to my mother, Mrs. Janie Wilson.

With all my love, to all my grandchildren and my great-grandson.

CONTENTS

INDEX OF PHOTOS USED

INTRODUCTION

I'm about to tell you a story, a story of life and crime, a story of drugs and alcohol and prostitution. This is a true story. In many ways, it is a tragic story, but it has a happy ending. Although life was not good to me and men did me great evil, God saved me and healed me. For that I am deeply grateful, and it is to glorify Him that I write this story.

Pearl Keith
Morgantown, West Virginia

Pearl Keith

Chapter 1

The Evil Influences in Our Little World

My three brothers and I grew up on "the Hill" in Pittsburgh, Pennsylvania. Our mother had married very early in life, at fourteen, and had come to Pittsburgh from South Carolina. Her life was very hard. Her husband left her, and she was forced to raise us the best she could.

At times we wandered the streets, seeking help, but then one day someone told Ma that she was eligible to apply for welfare. I remember going to the welfare office with her, and I remember that the lady asked her a lot of questions.

"The Hill" was not a very healthy place

for children to grow up. Drugs and crime were all around us, and as children we saw people being killed. So after Ma began to receive the help she sought from the welfare office, we were able to move off "the Hill" onto Wiley Avenue. It was better than "the Hill," but it was far from a good atmosphere for us children.

Ma's brother, Benny Raysor, was in the Mafia, and he dealt drugs, principally heroin and cocaine. He started out with a shop known as Benny's Shoeshine Place, where he dispensed liquor. Later he had a place called the Green Door where people danced and drank. It was open all hours of the night.

Eventually, Uncle Benny had his lieutenants who distributed drugs for him. Some covered the North Side of Pittsburgh, while others covered the South Side, the East Side and the West Side.

We moved again, this time to Frankstown Avenue, and there I saw sights that became deeply imbedded in my memory and affected my development. The area

Pearl Keith

was filled with prostitutes, pimps and players. I could see them from my window. I didn't know any better than to think these people were having fun, so I decided early in life that I would pattern my life after them. ❁

My grandmother, Pearl Bookheart

CHAPTER 2

A GODLY INFLUENCE

Not every influence in our lives was evil. Our grandmother, Pearl Bookheart, was a good woman, a godly woman. She worked at a nursing home called Leech's Farm. Even after it was discovered that she had cancer, she still tried to work, and she never stopped praising God.

Her influence was most felt at Thanksgiving and Christmas. She would come to our house and bring us things our mother could not get us. Grandma Bookheart was very gracious to do all that she could to make our lives more pleasant.

Toward the end of her life she came to stay with us. I once confided to her that something seemed to be following me, particularly every time I went up the steps. I ran because I was afraid. She said to me, "Sweetheart, when I close my eyes and go be with the Lord, don't worry about anything ever following you again. Nothing will follow you after that."

Every day when I came home from school I would run up the stairs to see how Grandma was. She would always have her eyes toward the wall and would be calling on Jesus. She believed in the power in that name and called on it continually.

One day I came in from school and started up the steps, but I did not feel the need to run. I was no longer afraid. Nothing was following me. It came to me then that Grandma was dead. That hurt me because I had been much closer to her than I was to my own mother.

With that thought in mind, I did run the rest of the way up the steps, and there I saw Grandma. Her eyes were fixed on the corner where she had usually seen the Lord, and her mouth was opened in the final praise she would utter here on this

Pearl Keith

Earth. There had been power in her hands, and no one could deny that it was a miracle how God had eased her pain in the final stages of cancer. Now she was gone from our lives forever. ❁

CHAPTER 3

A LIFE OF DRUGS AND PROSTITUTION

Uncle Benny and our mother went out to bury Grandma. Our older brother went along, but Leon and myself were not allowed to go. They gave her a very simple burial, and we went back to life as usual.

The police were after Uncle Benny because of his drug activities. He had bought two houses on Hamilton Avenue and some others up on "the Hill." He had a lot of money from his drug sales, and he used it now to hire a lawyer, Bird Brown, to try to get him off.

When his day in court arrived, Uncle Benny was sentenced to five to ten years

Pearl Keith

in Western Penitentiary. When he heard the
sentence, he cursed the judge, and the
judge doubled his sentence to ten to
twenty years.

Ma and I would go visit Uncle Benny
in jail. I felt so sorry for him. In time, however, I became addicted to the same drugs
he had been dealing. I couldn't bring myself to tell him about it, but through par-
tying and drinking, I had little by little
given my life over to alcohol, drugs and
sex.

It began very early, when I was about
twelve or thirteen. We would go to Uncle
Benny's place and drink and dance. By the
time I was fifteen, I was already into prostitution to make money for what I wanted
in life.

My serious addiction began when I was
about twenty. I didn't like reefers (mari-
juana) because they made me laugh and
they made me eat a lot, so I quickly moved
on to cocaine and heroin. After I got
hooked on hard drugs, my life of prostitu-

tion and theft supported my habit. I occasionally did uppers, downers, valiums, speed and crack. Whatever came along, I did it. I was deeply addicted to drugs for the next twenty-seven years, and consequently my life was a shambles. ❊

Chapter 4

Ups and Downs

I thought I might never be free from heroin and cocaine. Many of my friends died from it. Even the methadone treatment being offered to addicts killed some. Eventually, I was able to get free from the heroin and cocaine for a time, although I had to stay on methadone for years.

Growing up, I had never imagined I would become a drug addict. We had been put out of the houses we lived in so many times that I vowed I would work hard and never be put out on the streets again. Now that I was free of drugs, I got a job and eventually I bought a house, married and had a son. (I had given birth to a daughter some years before, and Mother had raised her.)

Life at our house was still chaotic. I was one day up and the next day down. I was very weak when it came to resisting my addiction. Sometimes I would look up in the window and say, "Lord, help me." I knew that I was not what He wanted me to be, but I also knew that I desperately needed Him.

I would often quote the 23rd Psalm:

The LORD is my shepherd; I shall not want. He maketh me to lie down in green pastures: he leadeth me beside the still waters. He restoreth my soul: he leadeth me in the paths of righteousness for his name's sake. Yea, though I walk through the valley of the shadow of death, I will fear no evil: for thou art with me; thy rod and thy staff they comfort me. Thou preparest a table before me in the presence of mine enemies: thou anointest my head with oil; my cup runneth over. Surely goodness and mercy shall follow me all the days of my life: and I will dwell in the house of the LORD for ever.

Pearl Keith

I was determined that I would somehow overcome my weaknesses and someday *"dwell in the house of the LORD for ever."* Some might think that a person who has lived in drug addiction and prostitution could never seek the Lord, but it is not true. I needed Him, and I needed Him desperately.

The marriage did not go well. My husband was more interested in women, Cadillacs and the wild life than he was in me. Life took a downward spiral, and I soon found myself in the county jail. Still, I was looking up to the Lord and saying, "Lord, help me."

I had met a lady minister named Rev. Agnes M. Turks and had sometimes gone to her house to seek her help. She had been kind to me in many ways, often helping me get back and forth to the hospital when I was ill. Rev. Turks had told me that I did not need to prostitute myself or steal to support my drug habit. She spoke of the greatness of God and His ability to deliver me out of everything. He could just take it all away from me, she said.

At the time Rev. Turks told me these things, I had very little faith, but now I thought of her when I was in the county jail. I called her and asked her to help me get out. "Baby," she said to me, "you've got to learn to trust the Lord."

Those were words that I didn't particularly want to hear at the moment. My focus was on getting out of jail, but I sensed that she was right. God was my only hope.

When I got back to the cell, I got on my knees and asked the Lord to help me. I surrendered to Him. I said, "Lord, if You help me, I will serve You. If You get me out of here, I will do the right thing." I made it much stronger this time, "Lord," I prayed, "if You help me just one more time, I will serve You till I die." And I meant it.

My resolve proved not to be nearly as strong as my intention, for I did get out, and no sooner was I free than I turned my back on the Lord and sought drugs. I also went right back to my life of prostitution and thievery to support my habit.

My house was on Fram Street and the

next street over was called Hell Street. I shot some drugs that night, and I over-dosed on heroin and cocaine. I was able to make it to a church on Hell Street where they were having a service, and bursting in through the doors, I pleaded with them to help me. They prayed for me, and very soon I felt better.

I got back on the methadone treatment, determined to do the right thing, but it seemed that Satan had his grips on me. As much as I tried, I could not seem to get it right — even to save my life.

Many addicts congregated at my house on Fram Street to shoot up and get high. A nurse would sometimes steal morphine from a local hospital and give it to us. We used whatever we could get our hands on. Now I spent everything I had on drugs, selling all my furniture and appliances.

Soon I developed a heart infection known as endocarditis. I remember my brother coming up the stairs and saying to me, "I give up on you, and I put you in the hands of the Lord."

"What do you mean by that?" I asked him.

He told me there was no hope for me, that he had given me to God, and he left.

I had hit rock bottom. There was nothing left in my house besides the bed. I had no running water, and I was very ill. I called the hospital and asked to be admitted. ❁

CHAPTER 5

HITTING ROCK BOTTOM

An ambulance was sent to get me. This was nothing new. I had been in and out of hospitals many times. I had gone through countless rehab programs. For a time, I had even been sent to a psychiatric institution. I had been having a lot of pain, and doctors could not determine what was causing it. They finally came to the conclusion that it was all in my mind. It was an awful feeling to tell someone you were hurting and hear them say that it was all in your mind. My pain was very real.

Now my lungs had collapsed, but because they knew in the emergency room that I was an addict, they didn't take me seriously. They left me sitting in the hallway for a long time, then they sent me back home. I had never been made to feel more like worthless trash.

Later I called another ambulance and was taken to University Hospital, where they discovered the collapsed lung. They told me that I could sue the other hospital because they had put my life at risk. I went to see a lawyer about it, but he told me that because I was a drug addict, no one would take me seriously. I would first have to go through rehab again, then stay clean for a good while before we could think of launching such a suit. I decided I didn't care about the lawsuit. All I wanted to do was to get myself straightened out.

When I got out of the hospital I began a course with NA (Narcotics Anonymous) and AA (Alcoholics Anonymous), hoping that my life would get better. It only grew worse, and I was soon back in the hospital to be treated for the endocarditis.

One day I was watching Pat Robertson on television. He invited those who wanted to be changed to accept Christ into their lives, and I did. I prayed and asked the Lord to save me and told Him that if He meant business with me, I meant business with Him.

Not long afterward, God sent a white lady from West Virginia to the hospital. She had reserved a suite, but when she got there her suite was taken. She asked at the desk if there was another room she could get into and was told that the only available room was with a black lady who smoked. (Even though I had endocarditis, I was still smoking.)

When I first saw this lady, I was duly impressed. She had very fine clothes and diamond jewelry.

"What's your name?" she asked me.

"Pearl," I answered.

"My name is Donna," she said. "I'm glad to meet you."

"Well, I'm glad to meet you too," I answered.

"Do you think we'll get along?" she asked.

"We'll get along just fine," I answered

her, "as long as you take those diamonds and all your money and put it all in the hospital safe." I was a recovering addict and I didn't trust myself with her valuables. ✿

CHAPTER 6

A GLIMPSE OF HOPE

They put me back on methadone and said that I would have to stay on it for another year. I didn't really want to because I knew that it, too, was addicting. Once you are on it, it's not easy to get off, but I reluctantly agreed. I had to get free of drugs again.

A friend, a drug dealer, came to visit me in the hospital one day and brought heroin and cocaine to offer me. It seemed that God was on one shoulder and the devil was on the other, and they were competing for my soul. The devil was saying, "Go ahead. Put that drug in the IV."

God was saying, "No. Don't do it. I set you free."

God won this time. I picked up the phone, pretending to call security, and my "friend" quickly left.

Donna and I became close friends and before she left the hospital, she asked me if I would like to come to Morgantown, West Virginia, to live with her. I had been praying about leaving Pittsburgh and going somewhere where I didn't know anyone and no one knew me. I felt that I could no longer live in Pittsburgh and remain free of drugs. I knew the town too well. I knew just where to get drugs. I knew just what to do when I wanted to turn a trick to get money. I knew just what to do when I wanted to steal. I asked God to take me away from Pittsburgh so that I could turn my life around.

I called my probation officer and explained the case and secured his agreement for me to move to Morgantown and try to make a new life for myself. Two weeks later, Donna came with her maid to get me and take me back home with her. She and her husband Kyle owned some

land in Independence, West Virginia, and
their home in Morgantown. I was joyous
over this divine intervention in my life,
and yet I was apprehensive. This woman
did not know me all that well. I had not
told her everything about myself. I was an
addict off the streets. Did she know what
she was getting herself in for? Would this
work?   ❀

CHAPTER 7

TESTS AND TRIALS

West Virginia was very different from Pittsburgh, and since I didn't know anyone, I had a lot of time on my hands. If there were drugs in Morgantown, I didn't know where they were. I was isolated. This was both wonderful and terrible for me.

Another thing that bothered me was that I never saw any black people. They were surely around, but I never came in contact with them. This bothered me. I had grown up with black people and spent my whole life with them. Now, everyone I saw was lily white.

Although Donna and her family were very kind to me, I soon found myself resentful and feeling like a prisoner. Their daughter was only eighteen, yet she enjoyed many liberties. They were treating me, a woman in her forties, like a child. I was accustomed to my liberties, but they were trying to protect me from myself.

Finally one day I called Rev. Turks, told her about my situation and asked if she could visit me in Morgantown. In my heart I was planning to go back with her. She came down and spent a week with me. She encouraged me not to complicate my parole by returning to Pittsburgh. This was God's wisdom.

In the meantime, I met another lady at a church called Powerhouse of Deliverance. Pat was young and ran a townhouse. I liked her very much and decided to move and live with her. This was against my probation agreement, and I couldn't be sure that a warrant would not be issued for my arrest. At Pat's place, I could pray all day long and seek the Lord.

God was being very good to me. When I had arrived at Donna's house, my teeth needed serious attention. They sent me to a dentist, Dr. Gokey, who made teeth for me and did not charge me.

I came to West Virginia with a single pair of socks, and both of them had holes in them. Now, again, I needed money. I was able to get some government assistance through the Drug and Alcohol Act. Then Pat wondered if I might qualify for a SSI pension and helped me apply for it. In time, the assistance was granted. I had been spending hours each day praising God and asking Him to make it possible for me to get my own place. I sensed that He had a plan for my life. He had not brought me all this way to abandon me.

Pat helped me to find a one-bedroom apartment, and I did my shopping with food stamps. The Lord was helping me through all the tests and trials. ❁

CHAPTER 8

RECOVERING WHAT WAS LOST

I had lost custody of my son some years before, and the next thing I began to pray about was for the Lord to help me get him back. Soon after I had gotten myself established with Donna's family, they began to take me to Mars, Pennsylvania, to visit my son in a home there. On our way back to Morgantown they told me they were sure I would one day get my son back.

A couple who encouraged me in this regard was Pastor David of Cheat Lake Baptist Church and his wife Sheila. They told me to have faith to believe that I would get my son back. When I said that I didn't have that faith, Pastor David said that he would believe for me, and he did.

Once I had established myself, I began proceedings in Juvenile Court in Pittsburgh to have my son returned to my custody. During the proceedings, the judge told me that he was very pleased that I had turned my life around and wanted my son. He said that most drug addicts never returned to reclaim their children. He asked my son what *he* wanted to do, and my son said he wanted to go home with me. In the end, he did move to West Virginia to live with me, and I was very happy about that.

He told me later that I had embarrassed him many times during the years I was on drugs. He had been forced to go to school sometimes in dirty clothes. When I could no longer care for him, he had gone to live with his grandparents, but things had not gone well there either. He rebelled against them, and they beat him with coat hangers. He showed me the marks he still bore.

I was glad to have him once again under my care, and I was glad that I was now a fit mother for him. He stayed with me several years, before establishing his own life in nearby Westover.   ❈

CHAPTER 9

A DESIRE TO HELP OTHERS

After my son came to live with me, I had many more requests to make of the Lord. For one, we were living in a one-bedroom apartment, and I was asking Him for a larger place. Another reason I wanted more space was that I wanted to help others. I suddenly had a great desire to minister to others, to help other people, as I had been helped. One of those I was led to help was my former husband. He had been on drugs for many years and had eventually been convicted of theft and sent to the same penitentiary Uncle Benny had gone to. While he was there, he tried to kill himself.

Speaking of Uncle Benny, he had served

nineteen years and eleven months when one day they found him dead in his cell. Before he died, I was told, he had gone to the prison chapel and given his life to God. I was happy to hear it.

Before God delivered me I could not say for certain that he would deliver my husband, but after I was free, I knew that he could be free too. Now that I was free of the heroin, the cocaine, the uppers and downers and valium and all the rest (and was even free of the methadone), I knew what God could do. Now that I was walking on water like Peter did, I knew that others could do it as well. By refusing to look at my circumstances and keeping my eyes on Jesus, I was able to overcome. Now I knew that this blessing was for others. I had been so bound that I thought I could never be free, but God was faithful and just to perform His Word. He brought me out. He delivered me. He placed my feet on solid ground, and He told me to stand.

My husband was released on methadone, and I took him to West Virginia and tried to help him get his life together. In the end, it was more than I could handle. His long years of taking drugs caused him some mental problems, and I eventually had to place him in a group home in Pittsburgh, where he could get the professional help he needed. He did get better and later called me to thank me for what I had done to help him.

My mother was getting older and I wanted to bring her to West Virginia and care for her. She was all alone in Pittsburgh, and I was afraid that she would be robbed or even shot and killed if she stayed there. At first, she said she didn't want to come with me. We had never had a close relationship, and she was afraid she might lose her income if she went out of state. I kept praying for her to come, and in time God honored my desire and sent her to me. Since Ma moved to West Virginia, we have developed a very good relationship.

I was also able to help my daughter, taking her and her two small children home with me. I could look at her and see everything that I had done with my own life. I had brought a curse upon my family, and I was determined to break that curse.

Only God could help me do it, I knew, so I spent much time in prayer and supplication. I wanted God's will for our lives.

❁

CHAPTER 10

A STEP BACK COST ME

God is faithful and just to do what He said He would do. He sends forth His Word, and it does not return to Him void. It accomplishes what He sent it to do. I was thanking the Lord for what He was doing in my life. I was thanking Him because He brought me through so many trials and tribulations. I was thanking Him because He had been so good to me. Truly He is a good God. His Word had taught me that if I kept my eyes on Him and I remained in His will, He would keep me in perfect health.

I had believed Him to get me out of Pittsburgh and take me to a new place where I could have a new life, and He had done it. He was honoring all my prayers and doing everything He said He would do.

Then I met a man ... and everything changed. This man was not saved and was attending Alcoholics Anonymous, but I had always felt the need of a man in my life and was sure that this one would fill the void I felt. I asked God to let me marry him, for I was sure I needed someone.

I thought I was still married to my first husband and that I would need a divorce in order to marry this man, but when I began to inquire I learned that I had applied for a divorce years before, and it had been granted. In my drugged state, I had forgotten those details. I'm sure I must have forgotten many other things too.

What a horrible slave master drugs are! I had been so engrossed in my life of drugs that often I would not bathe for weeks at a time. Eventually, the smell even bothered me, and I got tired of that life. Thank God for freedom in Jesus!

Marrying an unsaved man proved to be

a big mistake. Before long he was molesting someone dear to me. When I found out, I picked up a knife and was determined to kill him. He fled to another part of the state. Later, I wrote him and asked him what had possessed him to do such a thing. He answered me. I turned his letter over to the police and he was arrested and convicted for his crime and got five years to fifteen.

I was devastated by all of this and had to begin climbing back up the spiritual hill. I had obviously married outside the will of God for fleshly reasons, and I had reaped the ugly fruit of my error. Flesh is a monster. It wants what it wants when it wants it, and then we suffer the consequences.

Although I had made a mistake, God had not forsaken me. He was still dealing with me and still working with me. He is so good, and nothing we can do can change that fact. What He says He will do, He will do.

I eventually forgave the man. I knew

that if I was unwilling to forgive him, God could not forgive me. I had a long way to go. I could say with the Apostle Paul:

> *Brethren, I count not myself to have apprehended: but this one thing I do, forgetting those things which are behind, and reaching forth unto those things which are before, I press toward the mark for the prize of the high calling of God in Christ Jesus.*
>
> Philippians 3:13-14

CHAPTER 11

PROGRESS

In 1999 I had sufficiently recovered that a minister's license was bestowed on me to help others entrapped in drug and alcohol abuse. I had started going to a church called Salvation Praise Ministries, and they granted me this privilege. I had been very intent on getting into the ministry, and God had brought it to pass.

Pastor Turks, who had helped me so much through the years, also moved from Pittsburgh to Morgantown, and her presence became very important to my future. She had a child named Hal who had cerebral palsy. Doctors had said that he would never be able to walk, that he had only half a brain. I had known him in Pittsburgh and knew that he was severely afflicted.

Pastor Turks, however, had refused to give up on Hal. She loved that boy and prayed fervently for him, believing that he would one day be well. When I went there to help Pastor Turks move, I was amazed to see how well Hal was doing. He was now fourteen years old, and God had done an amazing thing for him. What a testimony of God's power! We moved them into a place my daughter had been occupying.

I moved several times myself over the years, always asking God to give me a permanent place to stay. By the time Pastor Turks came to Morgantown, I was living in a place in Cheat Lake. It had taken me years to get there. I was unable to get HUD assistance, so I needed the Lord's help. My income was very limited.

One day God told me to go downtown and sit in the courthouse square and He would send someone to meet me who had my home. I went downtown at noon that next day with an expectancy in my spirit.

Pearl Keith

In the square I met a man named Vincent who had a trailer for sale. I didn't have any money to pay on a trailer, but somehow we came to a written agreement. I got my trailer, and Mother and I moved in. God had once again proven His faithfulness to us. ✿

Rev. Agnes M. Turks

Chapter 12

Affliction

Through the years, I suffered numerous afflictions, many of them caused by my longstanding abuse of drugs and alcohol. I had hepatitis C and had to take interferon. I had sclerosis of the liver. I had a plate put in my left ankle because of getting gangrene. I had cataracts, glaucoma, diabetes and high blood pressure. I even had two permanent holes in my groin caused by the drug use.

Once I began to have terrible pain and could not imagine what was wrong with me. I was taken to the hospital, and tests revealed that I had gallstones. Fortunately, the gallstones were treatable by laser, and I recovered.

Just a year later, however, I began to suffer again. This time it was more serious. I was having heart problems again. I asked God to deliver me, and He did.

Then a new suffering came to me. For three years I was in devastating pain, pain that I would not have wished upon my worst enemy. One day I was putting something in the microwave oven when I felt a sharp pain in my breast. I examined myself and discovered two lumps. I was immediately devastated by the thought of cancer. I could not erase from my memory the sight of my grandmother suffering so terribly with it. I got in my car and drove to Westover to tell my daughter-in-law. She told me not to worry, that it was probably nothing, but the next day I made an appointment to have a mammogram.

About a week later, when I got the mammogram results back, my worst fears were realized. I had cancer.

I had been diagnosed eight years earlier with cancer at Fairmont General Hospital, but I had prayed and asked God to heal me. When I went back, they were unable to find any cancer.

Now I was told to come to the doctor's office and to bring someone with me. I was attending Salvation Praise Ministries, and Bishop Robert Scott Dixon went with me to the doctor's office. The doctor who waited on me told me that I had no reason to be fearful. They could remove the lump surgically.

I was not at all happy with this outcome. I had prayed and prayed that I would not get cancer, and now I had cancer. The thing that I had greatly feared came upon me.

The morning I went in for surgery Pastor Turks and I read the Word of God and prayed together. She assured me that God could heal me, but I had known so many people who had died of cancer that I was afraid.

One thing I was grateful for. Many of those I had known who died from cancer were not saved and had no assurance of eternal life. I had harbored my own doubts, but I had gone to spend some time in the home of Pastor Turks, and she had counseled and prayed with me. She also baptized me (in her bathtub), and I did everything else I knew to do to be ready. I had the assurance that if anything went wrong, I would go to be with the Lord.

Pastor Turks accompanied me to the hospital, and my family later met me there. I was disappointed that my Bishop was unable to come.

I was so terrified of cancer that I actually prayed before the operation that I would not survive it. I wanted God to take me home. I had suffered so much pain that I felt it would be better to go on to Heaven.

While they were preparing me for surgery, they had difficulty finding a vein they could use. I had abused drugs for so many years that my veins were a mess. They finally decided to use a vein in my neck, but I overheard them say that if that vein didn't hold up, I might not make it.

They did what they called a "cutdown," and I could feel blood running over my body. *Maybe I will die and go to be with Jesus now,* I was thinking.

Pearl Keith

When I came to, everybody was still there waiting to see what would happen to me. I could feel that my breast was gone. That was not what devastated me most, however. I was devastated that I was still alive. I had wanted very much to die that day. Now that I was alive, I would have to make the best of it. ❀

CHAPTER 13

LIFE AFTER CANCER SURGERY

After my surgery, Ma and I went to live permanently with Pastor Turks. We pray together and read the Word of God together every day, and I cannot complain about God's decision to let me live. He always knows best.

Before I began to experience affliction, every time I was off drugs and doing well or out of jail, I would go right back to sin. Affliction has been good for me. It has caused me to seek God more fully. If affliction had not come to me, I might not have been saved.

I encourage those who read these pages to love the Lord with all your heart. Do as the Scriptures teach:

Pearl Keith

*Trust in the LORD with all thine heart;
and lean not unto thine own under-
standing. In all thy ways acknowledge
him, and he shall direct thy paths.*

Proverbs 3:5-6

What we suffer in this life is not really important. What is important is the eternal destination of our souls. We must spend eternity in Heaven with Jesus. The Apostle Peter wrote to the church:

*Wherefore gird up the loins of your
mind, be sober, and hope to the end for
the grace that is to be brought unto you
at the revelation of Jesus Christ; As
obedient children, not fashioning your-
selves according to the former lusts in
your ignorance: But as he which hath
called you is holy, so be ye holy in all
manner of conversation; Because it is
written, Be ye holy; for I am holy. And
if ye call on the Father, who without
respect of persons judgeth according to*

*every man's work, pass the time of your
sojourning here in fear.*

1 Peter 1:13-17

The Lord has said of us:

*But ye are a chosen generation, a royal
priesthood, an holy nation, a peculiar
people; that ye should shew forth the
praises of him who hath called you out
of darkness into his marvellous light.*

1 Peter 2:9

Each of us has an appointment with
God, a day in which we will surely leave
this Earth. Every last one of us will eventually die. It's up to us, while we yet live,
if we will live for God or we will live for
the devil. I, for one, choose to live for God.

Even though I have been afflicted, I tell
myself that I am healed, because the Word
of God declares it to be so. Still, at some
point, this body must return to the dust.
My hope is that I am safe in Christ and
will dwell eternally with Him.

58

Pearl Keith

I thank God for Pastor Agnes Turks and her ministry. She is a great woman of faith. Every Sunday she travels back to Pittsburgh to fulfill her pastorate at Faith Temple where many members count on her spiritual leadership. Many of the people she ministers to are greatly afflicted. Some of them have difficulty breathing, some are on kidney dialysis, some have cancer, and some, like Sister Catherine, have heart problems.

I so admire these people and how they press their way to the church every week believing God for help. And I thank God for making me part of His ministry and not the devil's, and I'll serve Him this time for ever. It is a joy to serve the Lord in this way and to do His will. ❀

Chapter 14

The Welfare of Your Soul

My principal concern in writing this book has been to speak to the heart of those who are living their life without God. I pray that this very day you will seek His deliverance. Do not risk leaving this world without having accepted the Lord Jesus Christ as your personal Saviour.

God loves you, and He doesn't want you to open your eyes and find that you are in Hell because you neglected Him until it was too late. Start today walking according to His Word and His purpose, and do it while you are yet alive because we cannot praise the Lord from the grave. We cannot do His work when we are dead.

I speak today to drug addicts, alcoholics, prostitutes and anyone else who does not know my Lord. I urge you to consider Him today. Choose life, and you will live. Choose God, and you will be delivered from all your sinful ways and bad habits, just as I was delivered. Let Him set your feet on the solid rock, so that you can stand against the evils that surround you.

In closing, I just thank God for His goodness, I thank Him for His grace, and I thank Him for His mercy to me. *Drugs, Alcohol, and MEN KILLED ME, then GOD HEALED ME.*

Amen!

OH, HOW SWEET IS A MOTHER'S LOVE!

To my mother so kind.
She is sweet and loving
Also she has been praying for me
For over twenty years.

She is still the love of my life.
And this is true love
Because you only get one mother.
My son and daughter become second.

My mother knows how to love.
She didn't always, but now she does.
We went through the hard times.
And she is still beside me.

Oh, how sweet is a mother's love.

(Psalm 27)

— Pearl Keith

WORLD, DO YOU KNOW?

World, do you know that Christ was
born to save us from our sins?
World, do you know that if you'll ac-
cept Him, He'll give you peace within?
World, do you know that Christ died
for you, and then He rose again?
Do you know that He's the Prince of
Peace and Wonderful Counselor,
He's the King of kings and our Lord?

World, do you know that Christ was
born to save us from our sins?
World, do you know that if you'll ac-
cept Him, He'll give you peace within?
World, do you know that Christ will
be your Friend?
World, do you know?

— Pearl Keith

(inspired by God through Jovetta Jones)